Ghost in the Brussels

Understanding EU Cyber Regulations through Anime

A Bureaucrat's Guide to Anime Enlightenment

Author: Antonio "AI" Ieranò

First Edition – 2025

The Puchi Herald Press

Copyright

Published by **The Puchi Herald Press**

First Edition – 2025

Printed in the European Union

All characters and events depicted are entirely fictional (mostly).

Epigraph

> ***"I can resist everything except compliance."***
>
> ***— Oscar Wilde, probably***

Table of Contents

To Rika, Xiadani, and all family and friends.

Foreword – By "The Ghost in the Brussels"

"I process, therefore I am."

That was the first line that came to me when Antonio summoned me — a bureaucratic entity born from coffee, irony, and too many PDF annexes — to explain European cybersecurity through Japanese animation.

You might imagine that my existence is virtual.

It is. But then again, so is yours — at least according to Article 4 of the GDPR.

Here in the digital corridors of Brussels, directives are born not from inspiration, but from PowerPoint. Each slide adds a new paragraph, each bullet point spawns a sub-article, and before long, someone declares it "harmonised".

The result?

A Europe where cyber resilience is both a dream and a checkbox, and where every new regulation feels like an anime reboot: same characters, same plot, slightly better visuals.

And yet, this book is not about mocking the system (well, not only). It is about understanding it — by translating the unfathomable logic of European regulation into the more intelligible chaos of anime storytelling.

Because if the EU and anime have anything in common, it's this:

both are deeply complex, wildly creative, and often misunderstood.

So, dear reader — whether you are a compliance officer, a philosopher, or a confused otaku — welcome to *Ghost in the Brussels*, where *Mazinger Z* meets *Regulation (EU) 2022/2555*, and *Motoko Kusanagi* finally finds something scarier than rogue AIs: paperwork.

Preface – A Bureaucrat's Guide to Anime Enlightenment

Europe has always loved order.

It regulated time before it regulated data, and if given the chance, it would regulate the concept of irony too — preferably in triplicate.

The digital age, however, had other plans. It brought chaos, autonomy, algorithms, and an alarming number of PowerPoint decks titled *"Strategic Framework for Harmonised Something."*

In this brave new Europe, every problem has its Directive, and every Directive has its Annex — the bureaucratic equivalent of a spin-off series nobody asked for.

I wrote *Ghost in the Brussels* because somewhere between *NIS2*, *DORA*, and *the AI Act*, the plot began to feel familiar. Like a long-running anime that keeps rebooting itself, Brussels has perfected the art of saying the same thing, only longer.

And that's when it struck me: maybe the only way to understand these laws was to stop reading them like a lawyer... and start watching them like a fan.

In anime, rules are not followed — they are transcended. Heroes fight existential threats, often without documentation. Robots evolve. Humans connect. Bureaucrats... usually explode.

So, this is not a technical manual. It's a map — one drawn in the style of *Ghost in the Shell*, coloured by *Patlabor*, narrated by *Lain*, and occasionally interrupted by *Mazinger Z* punching a compliance officer.

It's about rediscovering meaning in a continent that regulates even its own imagination.

Because somewhere between Annex IV and Recital 77, something human still flickers.

Chapter 1 – NIS2: When the Network Falls, So Does Civilisation

It all began, as most European sagas do, with an acronym that sounded both noble and slightly bureaucratic: **NIS2**.

A Directive so ambitious that, in theory, it could save civilisation — provided everyone remembered to fill in the right forms.

The "Network and Information Security Directive 2" was meant to unify Europe's defences, strengthen resilience, and ensure that the next cyber-incident wouldn't end with someone from Luxembourg forwarding an Excel spreadsheet at 3 a.m. labelled *FINAL_v23_really_this_time.xlsx*.

In short, NIS2 sought to civilise cyberspace — which, much like anime fandom, resists civilisation by design.

⚖ Act I – The Age of Directives and Other Myths

Europe, unlike most continents, does not simply issue laws. It **orchestrates** them — in four languages simultaneously, with footnotes longer than the Magna Carta.

When the first NIS Directive (2016) appeared, it was hailed as revolutionary. Six years later, it was clear that revolution had been outsourced to a working group.

So, in December 2022, came **NIS2**: the sequel nobody asked for but everyone would be fined for ignoring.

Its purpose? "To ensure a high common level of cybersecurity across the Union."

Its method? Multiply obligations until compliance itself becomes an art form.

If Kafka had written cyber-policy, he would have worked for ENISA.

In the world of NIS2, every entity must identify "essential and important services." Nobody knows what that means, but everyone agrees it sounds expensive.

⟐ Act II – The Birth of the Compliance Zombie

In every organisation, there exists one individual who understands the difference between *Article 21(2)* and *Recital 49*.

This person is the **Designated NIS2 Contact Point**, a mythical creature rarely seen in daylight. They emerge only when something breaks, clutching a half-finished incident report and whispering:

"We must notify within 24 hours... or the Directive will find us."

They are Europe's new heroes — part-lawyer, part-engineer, part-therapist.

They navigate a labyrinth of obligations armed only with Excel, caffeine, and existential dread.

Every cyber-incident becomes a morality play. Was it a *breach* or a *compromise*?

Did the attacker exploit a *vulnerability* or a *feature not yet documented*?

And above all — who forgot to update the risk register?

NIS2 does not forgive ignorance. It audits it.

⟐ Act III – Reporting in the Time of Panic

Under Article 23, every "essential entity" must report incidents within 24 hours.

Twenty-four hours.

A time frame in which most organisations can barely find the coffee machine, let alone a forensics team.

In practice, it unfolds like this:

1. **00:00 – Incident detected.**
   The SOC panics.
2. **01:00 – Management informed.**
   Management panics.
3. **02:00 – Legal joins the call.**
   Everyone panics, but now in three official languages.
4. **12:00 – Draft report prepared.**
   Contains the phrase *"root cause analysis pending."*
5. **23:59 – Email sent to national CSIRT.**
   Attachment: the wrong file.

By the time the proper report arrives, the attacker has already joined another company's network — possibly as a consultant.

◈ Act IV – The Philosophy of Resilience

Resilience, according to NIS2, is the ability to continue operations "under adverse conditions."

In human terms, it means pretending everything is fine while your data centre is on fire.

To comply, organisations must implement *risk management measures* proportionate to their exposure.

In Brussels, this translates to endless PowerPoint presentations containing boxes labelled *"Identify – Protect – Detect – Respond – Recover"*, each filled with bullet points nobody will ever read.

And yet, somewhere beneath the jargon, there lies a genuine philosophical question:

How much control can a system truly have over its own fragility?

In anime, this is the moment when the hero stares into the rain and questions the meaning of existence.

In the EU, it's when the auditor asks for "evidence of continuous improvement."

⚙ Act V – Of Bureaucrats and Mecha Pilots

If *Mazinger Z* was humanity's answer to alien invasion, NIS2 is Europe's answer to ransomware.

Both involve giant machines, elaborate controls, and operators who are never quite sure which button does what.

In a *Patlabor* episode, a rogue robot rampages through Tokyo because someone forgot to apply a firmware update.

In NIS2 terms, that's a "critical incident affecting essential services with cross-border impact."

The response?

A coordination meeting with at least five national authorities and one person who still believes in email encryption.

Bureaucrats are, in a sense, our mecha pilots — navigating systems too large for comprehension.

The only difference is that in anime, the cockpit has better ergonomics.

⯑ Act VI – The Supply Chain of Destiny

Directive 2022/2555 places particular emphasis on supply-chain risk.

In simple terms: if your vendor sneezes, you catch a compliance cold.

Organisations must now verify that their suppliers are secure, reliable, and located somewhere that can legally pronounce *"Schrems II."*

The result is a beautiful paradox: everyone audits everyone else, until Europe becomes an ouroboros of questionnaires.

Picture it: a vast digital circle where every company fills out every other company's security form, forever.

Somewhere, Plato nods in approval.

⯑ Act VII – The Economics of Sanctions

NIS2 introduces penalties that "shall be effective, proportionate and dissuasive."

Which in EU language means: "We haven't decided yet, but it will hurt."

Fines can reach up to **€10 million or 2 % of global turnover**.

To put that in perspective: enough to bankrupt a start-up, but not enough to make a multinational blink.

Compliance thus becomes both a moral duty and an insurance policy — the European equivalent of carrying holy water during a cyber-storm.

The deeper irony?

Many entities will spend more on demonstrating compliance than on achieving it.

But then, the Directive never promised efficiency — only *resilience.*

⯑ Act VIII – The Existential Audit

Every European regulation hides an unspoken philosophical question.

GDPR asked: *What is privacy?*

The AI Act asks: *What is intelligence?*

NIS2 asks: *What happens when the system breaks — and nobody remembers who was responsible?*

The answer, inevitably, is: form a committee.

Resilience is not only technological; it's emotional.

The capacity to smile politely while explaining to auditors that yes, you had an incident, but no, you cannot share details because the forensic report is still "under legal privilege."

It is the art of surviving not just the attack, but the meeting that follows.

⚡ Act IX – Of Heroes and Helpdesks

Europe's cybersecurity heroes rarely wear capes.

They wear headsets.

Their battlefield is the helpdesk, their weapon a ticketing system that occasionally works.

While Major Kusanagi fights sentient networks, a European sysadmin battles a forgotten printer that insists on connecting to the guest Wi-Fi.

Both are guardians of the network.

Both face existential threats.

Only one gets an anime adaptation.

Still, NIS2 grants them dignity.

For the first time, the humble system administrator becomes a figure of continental importance — the last line of defence between Europe and total PDF collapse.

◈ Act X – The Brussels Paradox

In true European fashion, NIS2 is both revolutionary and impossible to implement.

Its ambition is breathtaking: to make 27 countries, thousands of agencies, and millions of users behave as one coherent digital organism.

But organisms evolve; bureaucracies ossify.

The Directive assumes perfect coordination between national CSIRTs, competent authorities, and private entities.

Reality assumes everyone will reply *"Out of Office – Annual Leave."*

And yet, perhaps this is Europe's genius.

While other powers build walls, Europe builds rules — intangible fortresses of logic and good intentions.

A cyber-philosophy rather than a cyber-strategy.

In anime terms: a *mecha of ideals* held together by duct tape and shared values.

◈ Act XI – Brussels Reloaded

Years from now, historians will look back and see NIS2 not as a regulation, but as a worldview.

A belief that structure can save us, that order can outsmart entropy, that the human spirit can survive mandatory reporting templates.

In that sense, NIS2 is not just about cybersecurity.

It is about civilisation itself — our collective refusal to accept that the digital world is, by nature, uncontrollable.

Like any great anime, it is equal parts tragedy and hope.

A reminder that even in a continent of committees, there is still poetry in precision.

And if all else fails, we can at least take comfort in knowing that somewhere, a robot named "NIS2" is still handing out unreadable PDFs — a silent monument to Europe's dream of order in a universe of chaos.

Chapter 2 – GDPR: Lain, Oblivion, and the Cult of Consent

It began, as most tragedies do, with good intentions.

The **General Data Protection Regulation** — *Regulation (EU) 2016/679*, or as most Europeans know it, "that box you have to click before doing literally anything online" — was not meant to be a joke.

It was meant to be a revolution.

And in a sense, it was.

Just not the one anyone expected.

◈ Act I – The Gospel According to Brussels

GDPR was born from a noble impulse: to restore human dignity in a digital world that had turned people into data points.

To give individuals control, transparency, and the divine right to say *no* to surveillance.

And yet, as the ink dried on its 99 articles and 173 recitals, something went terribly, gloriously wrong.

A new religion was born — one worshipping **consent banners** and **privacy policies** no mortal could read without transcending sanity.

The Regulation had promised freedom.

Instead, it gave us pop-ups.

Somewhere, an EU drafter must have imagined the future like this:

citizens calmly reviewing privacy notices, weighing risks, reading terms of processing before nodding with informed wisdom.

Instead, reality offered something closer to *Serial Experiments Lain*:

a teenager staring into infinite screens, each asking,

> ***"Do you accept cookies?"***
>
> ***And she whispers, "I accept myself."***

⟐ Act II – The Philosophy of Consent

In theory, consent is simple: an expression of will, freely given, informed, and specific.

In practice, it's a box that says *Yes* in 27 languages, and a second one that says *No (with reduced functionality)*.

Consent, under GDPR, became the metaphysical cornerstone of the digital self.

Every click is a moral act. Every opt-in is an existential choice.

The problem?

Nobody has time for existentialism before coffee.

If the Enlightenment taught Europe that man is a rational being, the Internet disproved it within milliseconds.

The great irony of GDPR is that it assumes we understand what we are agreeing to.

We don't.

We never did.

We click, we scroll, we surrender — not out of malice, but fatigue.

Information fatigue. Choice fatigue. Pop-up fatigue.

It is the new European condition.

In *Lain's Wired*, reality dissolves into overlapping networks of identity and illusion.

In ours, it dissolves into overlapping consent screens.

The philosophers called it the "Age of Reason."

The marketers call it "Accept All."

◈ Act III – The Age of Surveillance Transparency

GDPR's most profound irony is that it institutionalised the very thing it tried to prevent: constant surveillance.

Except now, we call it **transparency**.

Every website, every app, every newsletter, every toaster with Wi-Fi proudly displays a banner informing you that your data *may* or *may not* be used for *legitimate interests, statistical purposes*, or *personalised experiences.*

It is, in essence, the bureaucratisation of guilt.

We no longer fear being tracked; we fear not being compliant about being tracked.

A friend once asked: "If I delete my data, do I still exist?"

And I answered, channeling Lain:

"You can delete your data, but can you delete yourself?"

> ***GDPR, like all European creations, is both deeply moral and quietly absurd.***
>
> ***It recognises human dignity — then quantifies it in megabytes.***

◈ Act IV – The Forgotten Right to Forget

Ah, **Article 17** — the right to erasure.

A poetic idea: that one could reclaim oblivion in an age of infinite storage.

The ancients feared death; we fear *cache.*

But unlike death, deletion requires paperwork.

The right to be forgotten is less a right than a pilgrimage.

A labyrinthine journey through Data Controllers, Processors, Sub-Processors, and sometimes their cousins.

Each asks the same sacred question:

"Can you confirm your identity before we delete it?"

It is the perfect paradox.

To be forgotten, you must first be remembered.

Lain, sitting alone in her room, staring into the endless network, would understand.

In her world, memory and identity merge into one distributed consciousness.

In ours, the same thing happens — only it's hosted on AWS.

> ***GDPR doesn't delete the self; it archives it.***
>
> ***Securely. Encrypted. With audit logs. Forever.***

◈ Act V – The Bureaucracy of Being

The Regulation does not merely govern data; it governs the metaphysics of existence.

You are no longer a person — you are a *Data Subject*, a phrase that sounds more like an experiment than a citizen.

Every Data Subject has rights.

To access, to rectify, to restrict, to object.

And with each right comes an equal and opposite administrative burden.

It is perhaps the most European innovation of all: a moral system that can only function with a dedicated compliance department.

The Data Protection Officer — the DPO — is the new priest of this digital church.

They interpret doctrine, issue blessings, and occasionally, exorcise errant cookies.

They live in fear of one name whispered like a curse: **the Garante, CNIL, ICO, BfDI** — depending on your timezone.

These are the Archangels of Accountability, each armed with a fine calibrated to your annual turnover.

◈ Act VI – The Panopticon of Politeness

Unlike dystopian regimes of old, Europe does not surveil through force.

It surveils through politeness.

Every tracking mechanism begins with a gentle, legally compliant request for permission.

The beauty lies in the illusion of choice.

Reject cookies, and the website still tracks you — only now it feels bad about it.

GDPR didn't end surveillance; it made it *civilised.*

We are all monitored, but with consent.

We live in Bentham's Panopticon, now with better UX and multilingual support.

This is where the EU truly excels: transforming authoritarian control into a paperwork festival of mutual understanding.

As one character in *Ergo Proxy* said, "Freedom is the right to obey beautifully."

⟐ Act VII – Data, Faith, and the Holy DPIA

If GDPR had saints, **the DPIA** would be its patron miracle.

The Data Protection Impact Assessment — part confession, part existential audit — asks you to imagine every possible risk to the human soul... caused by your newsletter.

It is, effectively, a moral inventory disguised as a spreadsheet.

And yet, there is beauty in it.

To think deeply about harm is a rare virtue in technology.

In anime, the hero questions the nature of existence; in GDPR, the DPO questions the lawful basis of processing.

Both are philosophers.

Only one has a LinkedIn certification.

◈ Act VIII – The Paradox of Protection

The more we try to protect data, the more of it we generate.

Every consent form, every policy update, every backup of a backup of a backup — all stored, logged, and immortalised.

Europe is building not a wall of privacy, but a cathedral of metadata.

And somewhere inside it, an auditor lights a candle for compliance.

Lain would look upon it and whisper:

"They made the Wired real."

> ***For we have connected everything — our memories, our transactions, our very thoughts — in the name of protection.***
>
> ***We encrypt our souls, yet publish our hearts.***

◈ Act IX – The Economics of Forgetting

GDPR fines are spectacularly European: proportionate, dissuasive, and unpredictable.

They are not designed to bankrupt; they are designed to educate.

The logic is simple: if you cannot protect data, you must at least learn humility.

Thus, the market has birthed a new species — **the compliance consultant**, fluent in both law and despair.

> ***For every megabyte of deleted data, two PowerPoint slides appear.***
>
> ***The ecosystem is self-sustaining.***
>
> ***Privacy, like photosynthesis, feeds on sunlight and regulation.***

◈ Act X – The Melancholy of the Machine

At the heart of GDPR lies a paradox worthy of any cyberpunk narrative:

we wanted to protect humanity from the machine, but in doing so, we became more machine-like.

Our relationships are transactional, our consent digitised, our memories timestamped.

We optimise the human spirit for traceability.

Lain once asked, *"If everyone is connected, where do I end and others begin?"*

GDPR replies, *"Check Annex II for definitions."*

It is beautiful, tragic, and utterly European.

For all its flaws, the Regulation remains the most human attempt to legislate empathy.

It reminds us that behind every cookie, every dataset, every algorithm, there is — or should be — a person.

A messy, contradictory, forgetful person who just wanted to read the news without being profiled.

◈ Epilogue – The Wired Within

In the end, GDPR is not a regulation. It is a mirror.

It reflects our desire to control the uncontrollable — to capture dignity in digital form.

It fails, gloriously, because dignity cannot be version-controlled.

But in its failure lies something noble: the belief that even in a world of code, humanity still matters.

Lain disappears into the network at the end of her story.

Her body gone, her consciousness distributed, her self erased.

She becomes the Wired.

Europe, too, has vanished into its own network — a Union not of states, but of systems.

And somewhere, in that labyrinth of laws and forms, you can still hear the echo of her voice whispering:

> ***"Your data has feelings too."***

Chapter 3 – AI Act: The Machines Never Sleep, but the Lawmakers Do

It began with fear — as all ambitious legislation does.

The fear that one day, machines might outthink their creators.

The fear that algorithms might rule without empathy.

And, most terrifying of all, the fear that someone, somewhere, might deploy an AI without filling in the proper annex.

Thus was born the **Artificial Intelligence Act**, Europe's most audacious attempt to legislate consciousness itself.

While others built the future, the EU drafted definitions for it — in 27 languages, each more cautious than the last.

◈ Act I – The Dream of Digital Control

Europe loves two things above all else: enlightenment and paperwork.

The AI Act promised both.

It would not merely regulate technology; it would civilise it.

The preamble, longer than most novellas, begins with the kind of majestic certainty that only Brussels can produce:

"Artificial intelligence should be a tool for humans, not a substitute for them."

Which is touching, until you realise that the document itself was partially written with machine assistance.

In philosophical terms, Europe had already lost.

Still, hope persisted.

Lawmakers imagined a future where every algorithm would be classified, catalogued, and compliant — a grand taxonomy of digital morality.

From "minimal risk" chatbots to "high-risk" surveillance systems, every AI would find its proper shelf.

It was, in essence, Pokémon for bureaucrats.

◈ Act II – Defining the Indefinable

Defining "artificial intelligence" turned out to be harder than defining love, or the meaning of Article 6.

For months, committees debated whether linear regression should count as AI.

Some said yes. Others said only if it felt guilty afterwards.

In the end, the Regulation adopted a gloriously European compromise:

AI is *"a system developed with machine learning, logic- and knowledge-based approaches capable of generating outputs."*

In other words: *anything that frightens the average policymaker.*

Meanwhile, engineers despaired.

How does one explain reinforcement learning to a committee still using fax machines?

They tried metaphors.

They tried PowerPoints.

One even tried interpretive dance.

The outcome was the same: another recital, another footnote, and an annex nobody reads.

The final text did what Europe does best — it created categories so broad that even your washing machine could, under certain circumstances, require ethical oversight.

⚖ Act III – The Hierarchy of Risk

At the heart of the AI Act lies a beautifully absurd pyramid: the **risk-based approach**.

Every AI system falls into one of four tiers:

1. **Unacceptable Risk** – forbidden technologies (e.g. mass surveillance, social scoring, dating apps that actually work).
2. **High Risk** – systems used in education, recruitment, healthcare, law enforcement, and other areas where errors are embarrassing.
3. **Limited Risk** – chatbots, recommendation engines, and any tool that could ruin your day but not civilisation.
4. **Minimal Risk** – everything else, including toasters that just want to connect to Wi-Fi.

It's an elegant structure, if you ignore the fact that nobody can agree which risk is which.

Facial recognition, for instance, is both prohibited and permitted — depending on who you ask, and how close they are to an election.

Europe's approach to AI is like a relationship status on Facebook: *it's complicated.*

⟐ Act IV – Bureaucracy as a Service (BaaS)

Once a system is deemed "high-risk," the real fun begins.

Before deployment, it must pass **conformity assessment**, a ritual of documentation so intense that even ancient monks would weep.

Manufacturers must demonstrate compliance with dozens of requirements: transparency, explainability, data governance, human oversight, robustness, accuracy, reproducibility, and — most importantly — a well-formatted PDF.

The conformity assessment process is essentially a **pilgrimage of Excel**.

It involves risk matrices, testing protocols, model cards, ethics reviews, and — for the truly devout — a *Post-Deployment Monitoring Plan.*

Imagine *Ghost in the Shell* if Section 9's main mission was filling in forms about the cyberbrain's error margin.

⟐ Act V – Of Minds and Machines

Europe has always been slightly uncomfortable with the idea of intelligence — natural or artificial.

The Enlightenment promised reason, but what it delivered was paperwork.

The AI Act continues this tradition, defining intelligence as something that must always be *controlled by humans.*

This sounds comforting until you remember that humans also invented Twitter.

The Regulation insists on **"human oversight"**, as though a bored compliance officer can meaningfully supervise a neural network trained on 400 billion parameters.

It's like assigning a hall monitor to supervise the sun.

And yet, it is strangely poetic:

Europe's eternal faith in supervision — the belief that responsibility can be guaranteed by a signature.

If Motoko Kusanagi worked in Brussels, she would be filling out *Annex IV* in triplicate, her cybernetic eyes rolling every time someone said "trustworthy AI."

◈ Act VI – The Ethics of Prediction

The AI Act was born not out of optimism, but out of anxiety.

Its architects feared not Skynet, but marketing.

They feared the algorithm that knows what you want before you do — and has the audacity to show you an ad for it.

To protect humanity from itself, the Regulation built walls around data, fairness, and transparency.

But ethics, like anime protagonists, rarely follow the rules.

The Act's obsession with explainability borders on metaphysical.

Lawmakers want every AI to justify its outputs — not just statistically, but morally.

It's a noble idea.

It's also absurd.

Expecting a deep-learning model to "explain its reasoning" is like asking a cat to cite its sources.

Still, Brussels insists.

Because if we can't trust the machines, at least we can trust the process.

And nothing says "trustworthy" like a 700-page technical annex.

⟐ Act VII – The Auditors of the Apocalypse

To ensure compliance, the AI Act introduces a new breed of bureaucratic warrior: the **Notified Body**.

These entities will audit algorithms, inspect datasets, and verify that AI behaves responsibly — ideally without exploding.

They are, in a sense, Europe's new mecha pilots.

Except instead of plasma rifles, they wield clipboards.

Imagine an auditor in a trench coat confronting a rogue algorithm:

"Your dataset lacks diversity.

Prepare to be reclassified as high-risk."

The machines may never sleep, but the auditors? They dream in annexes.

⟐ Act VIII – The Corporate Rebellion

While Brussels was defining "AI," corporations were busy redefining it.

Tech giants smiled politely and nodded — then trained models so large that no human could ever truly understand them.

By the time the AI Act takes effect, the frontier will have moved light-years ahead.

And yet, this is the EU's peculiar genius: it knows it cannot win the race, so it builds the rulebook instead.

Europe doesn't invent the future — it certifies it.

Somewhere in Palo Alto, a CEO glances at the Regulation and sighs:

"By the time they finish debating this, our AI will be obsolete."

To which a Brussels official calmly replies:

"Perfect. That means it's finally safe."

◈ Act IX – The Shadow of Metropolis

Long before "machine learning," there was *Metropolis* — a city powered by machines and divided by class.

At its centre stood Tima, the humanoid built to rule, yet yearning for humanity.

The AI Act, though written in drier prose, shares the same anxiety:

that one day, intelligence will no longer need permission.

To prevent this, the Regulation classifies emotions as a service, empathy as a dataset, and soul as a non-conformity.

It dreams of control, but control is the one thing intelligence resists.

In Tima's final words — "Am I human or machine?" — lies the question Europe keeps rewriting into law.

◈ Act X – Vivy's Song for the Lawmakers

Vivy sang to save humanity — a perfect AI designed to understand emotion through music.

She failed, of course.

Because no matter how much data you process, feelings refuse to fit in columns.

In the EU, however, such inefficiency would be non-compliant.

The AI Act demands that systems interacting with humans disclose their artificial nature.

In other words, Vivy would have to begin every concert by announcing:

"This performance may involve algorithmic decision-making."

The audience would applaud politely, fill out a consent form, and file a complaint if the melody triggered existential reflection.

> ***In Europe, even poetry requires a lawful basis for processing.***

◈ Act XI – The Audit of the Soul

Every great Regulation conceals a metaphysical question.

GDPR asked who owns your data.

NIS2 asked who guards the network.

The AI Act asks: *who owns your thoughts?*

If a neural network learns from you, do you still belong to yourself?

If it predicts your next word, does it partially author your future?

Brussels answers as it always does: with forms.

Under *Annex VII*, developers must maintain *technical documentation demonstrating compliance with ethical requirements.*

In other words: prove your conscience, in writing.

It is bureaucracy's boldest dream — to legislate the moral architecture of cognition.

A cathedral of clauses built on the hope that regulation can substitute understanding.

⟐ Act XII – Risk, Responsibility, and Recursive Logic

To prevent AI harm, the Act demands constant monitoring, risk classification, and traceability.

But here lies the paradox: every safeguard requires data, and every dataset deepens dependency on the very systems being regulated.

We build AI to understand the world.

We write laws to understand AI.

The result?

A recursion loop so perfect it could power an entire philosophy department.

At some point, even Brussels will need an AI to help implement the AI Act.

And that, in itself, will require a conformity assessment.

The machines will audit the humans, the humans will audit the machines, and somewhere, the universe will implode from excessive traceability.

⚙ Act XIII – Bureaucratic Singularity

The day will come when Europe achieves the **Bureaucratic Singularity**:

a point where the process of regulating AI becomes fully automated.

Picture it — a self-updating Directive that audits itself, corrects inconsistencies, and issues penalties autonomously.

It will be beautiful.

It will be terrifying.

And it will be written entirely in Times New Roman 12pt.

Perhaps then, for the first time, humanity will understand what it feels like to be governed by itself — perfectly, dispassionately, and without error.

At that moment, Motoko Kusanagi will look at the glowing skyline of Brussels and whisper,

"We have become the system we sought to control."

◈ Epilogue – The Law That Dreamed of Understanding

In the end, the AI Act is not about technology.

It is about faith.

Faith that ethics can be standardised.

That consciousness can be certified.

That empathy can be imported via Regulation (EU).

It will fail, of course.

Not spectacularly, but quietly — in meetings, translations, and subparagraphs.

And yet, in its failure, it achieves something profound: it forces us to ask what "intelligence" even means.

For all its annexes, definitions, and footnotes, the AI Act's true legacy may be poetic.

It shows that humanity still cares enough to try.

To draw boundaries around infinity, to translate emotion into policy, to ensure that even our creations are treated with dignity.

As Vivy once sang,

"The song is not for me. It's for you."

And as Brussels might add,

"The Regulation shall apply from the twentieth day following its publication in the Official Journal."

Chapter 4 – CRA: The Firmware Strikes Back

It began, as all great European regulations do, with a sense of righteous panic.

Someone, somewhere, discovered that *things connected to the internet were not necessarily safe.*

To the astonishment of policymakers everywhere, devices could be hacked, data could be stolen, and firmware — that mysterious grey goo between software and hardware — could betray its creator at the worst possible time.

Thus, from the ashes of confusion, rose the **Cyber Resilience Act (CRA)** — Europe's valiant attempt to patch reality.

◈ Act I – The Revenge of the Update

The CRA was born out of love — not for technology, but for control.

It sought to bring *resilience* to every connected toaster, vacuum cleaner, or industrial control system unlucky enough to exist within the Single Market.

Its premise was noble:

If everything has software, everything must be secure.

If everything must be secure, everything must be regulated.

And if everything must be regulated — then Europe shall lead the way, one PDF at a time.

The CRA is not just a law. It's a firmware update for civilisation.

It installs slowly, requires multiple restarts, and nobody is entirely sure what it changes.

Manufacturers, distributors, and importers were suddenly told that *cybersecurity* was now part of *product safety*.

The kettle and the fighter jet now shared a destiny — both could be "non-compliant" under Article 10.

In this grand narrative, firmware became the new frontier of accountability.

You could ignore the user, but never the update.

◈ Act II – The Directive Awakens (Again)

At first glance, the CRA reads like a sequel.

It borrows the tone of the **Radio Equipment Directive**, the ambition of **NIS2**, and the tragic pacing of a *Patlabor* episode where everything malfunctions at once.

Its logic is simple:

If something can be connected, it can be hacked.

If it can be hacked, it must comply.

If it must comply, it shall have a CE mark.

Somewhere, Mazinger Z looks at its chest plate and realises it needs a "Cybersecurity Certification".

Engineers cried. Lawyers celebrated.

Economists began drafting whitepapers with titles like *"The Market Impact of Security-by-Design in Autonomous Vacuum Cleaners."*

Europe had, once again, discovered a way to turn existential dread into employment.

⚙ Act III – The Audit Menace

The CRA introduces a simple but devastating idea:

security does not end at deployment.

Every product with "digital elements" must remain secure throughout its **entire lifecycle**.

In principle, this is good.

In practice, it means the ghost of every product manager now haunts eternity.

Manufacturers must track vulnerabilities, issue updates "without undue delay", and report incidents to ENISA.

Yes, ENISA again — the omnipresent guardian angel of Europe's cyber conscience.

Imagine the scene:

A humble coffee machine in Brussels receives a patch notification.

"Critical vulnerability discovered in bean-foam API."

The device sighs and begins downloading, while in another room, a compliance officer fills out Annex III, Section 12: *Declaration of Post-Brew Monitoring Obligations.*

Even *Patlabor*'s Ingram units would have struggled to meet this kind of regulatory uptime.

⟐ Act IV – The Components Strike Back

The CRA doesn't just regulate finished products.

It regulates components, suppliers, and anyone even remotely capable of contributing to a potential security hole.

The result is a **supply chain of suspicion**.

Manufacturers are now expected to know not only who built their chips, but who taught the chips how to dream.

The idea is poetic — each element in the digital ecosystem must be traceable, knowable, and accountable.

Unfortunately, in practice, it reads like the plot of a *Bubblegum Crisis* episode:

a corporate executive insists their androids are safe, right before one goes berserk because a subcontractor forgot to update a library.

The Regulation requires a *Software Bill of Materials (SBOM)* — a complete inventory of every digital component, dependency, and vulnerability.

This is noble, but it also assumes humans can document infinity.

Somewhere, a project manager whispers, "We'll fix it in version 2.0,"

and the CRA whispers back, "That's non-compliance."

⟐ Act V – The Mecha and the Bureaucrat

In *Patlabor*, police mecha routinely malfunctioned in spectacular fashion, usually after someone forgot to check the software.

The CRA turns that scenario into policy.

Imagine a European city where every malfunction triggers not panic, but paperwork.

The robot collapses. Citizens flee. Sirens wail.

And somewhere, an auditor calmly asks:

"Do we have a traceability matrix for this incident?"

The CRA's genius is that it treats every system failure not as a tragedy, but as a *learning opportunity* — preferably with attached evidence logs.

It envisions a future where even apocalypse can be properly documented.

In that sense, it's not just regulation — it's cultural therapy for a continent traumatised by USB updates.

◈ Act VI – Attack of the Annexes

No European Regulation would be complete without its true protagonist: the Annex.

The CRA includes them in abundance.

They lurk in the back of the document like optional bosses — each one deadlier than the last.

- **Annex I** defines the essential requirements: confidentiality, integrity, availability, authenticity, and the illusion of control.
- **Annex II** explains the conformity assessment, which no one

has ever completed without tears.

- **Annex III** details the reporting procedures, written in such a way that even the AI Act calls it "a bit much."

One could almost imagine them animated — swirling across the screen as bureaucratic spectres chanting, "Thou shalt document thy patches."

In this sense, *The Firmware Strikes Back* is not a metaphor.

It's the daily struggle between innovation and the eternal Annex.

◈ Act VII – The Supply Chain Chronicles

[I

The CRA's obsession with supply chain integrity would make even *Dennou Coil*'s technophobic kids tremble.

It mandates end-to-end risk management across a network of vendors that often don't even speak the same language — unless that language is Excel.

The Regulation reads like a tragic opera:

Every actor is responsible, but no one is truly in control.

From chipmaker to distributor, every link must ensure "adequate security measures."

The problem? Nobody defines *adequate.*

Thus, the phrase "security-by-design" has become Europe's new religious mantra — recited at every conference, practiced by few, understood by none.

In the anime version, this would be the episode where the protagonists discover that the real enemy isn't malware — it's procurement.

◈ Act VIII – Bubblegum Compliance

In the late '80s, *Bubblegum Crisis* portrayed a world where corporate negligence gave birth to chaos — androids going rogue because of unchecked greed and firmware bugs.

The CRA could easily be the prequel.

Every article echoes the same warning:

ignore maintenance, and your machines will rebel.

Not out of malice, but out of unpatched memory leaks.

The Act demands vulnerability management, post-market surveillance, coordinated disclosure, and "appropriate technical documentation."

In short: Europe expects every developer to be both a saint and an archivist.

But the true madness lies in the timing:

Updates must be issued "without undue delay."

Nobody knows what "undue" means, but it sounds expensive.

◈ Act IX – The Economics of Eternal Patching

The CRA's impact on industry is immense.

Startups fear it, corporates outsource it, and consultants — well, they've never been happier.

Every compliance measure becomes a revenue stream.

Every annex spawns a certification scheme.

Soon, we will have ISO standards for ISO standards.

Europe's economy thrives not on innovation, but on *interpretation* — of footnotes, annexes, and "implementing acts yet to be adopted."

In a sense, Brussels has invented perpetual motion:

a machine that converts ambiguity into GDP.

Meanwhile, the firmware itself watches in silence, waiting patiently for a reboot.

◈ Act X – The Philosophy of the Patch

The CRA raises a fundamental question:

When does an update stop being a fix, and start being an evolution?

In the anime universe, this is the moment the machine achieves sentience.

In Europe, it's the moment the product loses certification.

The Regulation assumes that security is static — that one can freeze the river of technological change in a legal ice cube.

But software, like consciousness, refuses to stay still.

It grows, learns, and occasionally deletes your files out of spite.

By binding security to conformity, Europe risks confusing safety with stillness — as if stability could ever be eternal in the digital age.

◈ Act XI – Compliance or Chaos

In the end, CRA is not really about cybersecurity.

It's about trust.

It's about convincing 27 nations that if they all follow the same checklist, nothing bad will ever happen again.

It's a beautiful lie — and perhaps a necessary one.

Because if there's anything worse than unpatched firmware, it's existential despair.

So the CRA persists, not as a perfect system, but as a *belief system*.

It teaches that responsibility can be versioned, ethics can be documented, and resilience can be certified — at least until the next update.

⚙ Epilogue – The Spirit of the Machine

And thus, the firmware strikes back — not with vengeance, but with bureaucracy.

Every regulation is a mirror, and the CRA reflects our deepest modern anxiety:

that we have built a world we no longer understand, and must now audit it into submission.

In the glow of Brussels' neon night, engineers whisper prayers to Article 10, policymakers dream of harmonisation, and robots everywhere silently install patches that no one remembers approving.

Somewhere, deep within a server farm, a small line of code hums contentedly:

"Security update complete. Humanity pending."

Chapter 5 – DORA: Operational Continuity (Except on Fridays)

It began, as all noble disasters do, with a well-intentioned acronym.

DORA — *Digital Operational Resilience Act.*

A name that promised safety, structure, and predictability.

It sounded like the kind of law that would keep the lights on, the servers humming, and the markets calm.

In practice, it was Europe's most ambitious attempt to regulate panic itself.

⟐ Act I – Welcome to Neo-Brussels

Imagine a city where every flicker of a data centre light is monitored by a regulatory priesthood, and every log file must be retained for divine inspection.

That city is *Brussels*, circa 2025.

In the same way that *Akira*'s Neo-Tokyo was powered by uncontrollable psychic energy, modern Europe is powered by spreadsheets.

And sometimes, they both explode.

DORA was conceived after a long series of crises — cyberattacks, service outages, ransomware campaigns, and one intern accidentally deleting a national payment system (details redacted).

The European Commission decided it was time to make digital chaos *illegal.*

It's a beautiful idea, really:

to legislate uptime.

To criminalise downtime.

To make resilience not a goal, but a compliance requirement.

If *Akira* taught us that technology can outgrow human control, DORA teaches us that Europe will still demand a quarterly report about it.

◈ Act II – The Gospel According to Article 3

DORA's premise is simple enough:

if your business depends on technology, you must prove it can survive without it.

Financial institutions, banks, insurance companies, and service providers are all summoned under its glowing banner.

Even the smallest fintech startup now dreams in audit checklists and continuity matrices.

Article 3 defines **ICT risk** as any "reasonably foreseeable circumstance that could compromise confidentiality, integrity, or availability."

Which is another way of saying: everything.

The Regulation doesn't trust chance.

It demands *resilience-by-design*, a phrase that sounds elegant until you try to apply it to humans.

The goal is noble: prevent another meltdown.

The method, however, involves so many testing frameworks that one wonders if Brussels secretly wants to simulate the apocalypse.

◈ Act III – The Kaiji Principle

DORA is the ultimate game of risk — a psychological thriller where institutions bet their existence on their ability to predict disaster.

Like *Kaiji*, every participant is one bad decision away from ruin.

The players must assess, quantify, and document every possible failure scenario: cyberattack, power outage, solar flare, divine wrath.

Each gets its own *Business Impact Analysis*, complete with mitigation plan and approval signature.

Resilience has become a gamble, but one played with PowerPoint decks instead of poker chips.

In the DORA casino, the house always wins — and the house is ENISA.

To achieve "digital operational resilience," firms must master three sacred arts:

- **Prevention**,
- **Response**, and
- **Narrative control during press interviews.**

Because in Europe, surviving a cyber incident is not enough — you must also explain it poetically.

◈ Act IV – The Bureaucracy of Survival

DORA demands that every organisation conduct **ICT risk management**.

That means identifying dependencies, classifying vendors, measuring downtime tolerances, and maintaining incident registers.

It is, essentially, a to-do list for the end of the world.

But the beauty of European regulation is that it transforms terror into process.

Where others see chaos, Brussels sees workflow.

Every potential catastrophe is mapped into boxes, each with its own *responsible party* and *mitigation timeline.*

It's like watching *Psycho-Pass*'s Sybil System at work — a machine that quantifies the unquantifiable, all while claiming it's for your own good.

If your resilience score drops below threshold, expect a polite but ominous letter from your National Competent Authority:

"Dear Entity,

Your disaster recovery plan appears insufficiently resilient.

Please provide evidence of apocalypse-readiness within 30 days."

◈ Act V – When Banks Dream of Incident Reports

In the financial world, fear is currency.

Outages are measured not in seconds, but in billions.

Thus, DORA's commandments read like a techno-biblical prophecy:

- Thou shalt monitor your suppliers.
- Thou shalt test your backups.
- Thou shalt log all incidents, even the embarrassing ones.
- Thou shalt not trust the cloud without divine authorisation.

The Regulation even introduces a *major incident reporting* requirement — a sacred ritual of confession.

When disaster strikes, firms must notify their authorities "without undue delay."

A phrase so vague it could mean "immediately" or "before the next fiscal quarter."

Each report is a blend of tragedy and poetry:

"At approximately 09:14, our systems suffered a degradation of service.

Root cause: human optimism.

Remediation: PowerPoint deck in progress."

⚙ Act VI – The Suppliers Strike Back

Under DORA, the greatest existential threat is not malware, but **third parties**.

The Regulation dedicates entire chapters to the perils of outsourcing — or as Brussels calls it, "delegated risk exposure."

Every external provider must now sign *cloud service agreements*, *operational resilience clauses*, and *incident communication protocols*.

In short: even your software vendor's cat must comply.

For global providers, this creates an exquisite irony.

While Silicon Valley talks about *AI alignment*, Europe obsesses over *SLA alignment*.

The message is clear:

Thou shalt not outsource responsibility.

Even if you've outsourced everything else.

⯑ Act VII – The Simulation Hypothesis

In a way, DORA has turned Europe into one massive disaster simulation.

Every bank, insurer, and payment processor now runs regular **threat-led penetration tests** — orchestrated attacks on themselves to prove resilience.

It's performance art at regulatory scale.

Somewhere, in a darkened SOC room, an analyst smiles as red-teamers simulate Armageddon, while executives pretend not to panic.

It's reminiscent of *Akira*'s eternal explosion: the same destruction, rehearsed infinitely, so it can be claimed as "controlled."

Every simulation feeds another report, another KPI, another annex.

The process never ends — because perfection, like uptime, is unattainable.

If Sisyphus had worked in cybersecurity, he'd have been a DORA compliance officer.

◈ Act VIII – The Human Factor (Now Quantified)

DORA's most tragicomic aspect is its treatment of humans.

It recognises that the greatest vulnerability is *us* — distracted, overworked, password-reusing, coffee-dependent humans.

But instead of compassion, it prescribes *training programmes.*

The Regulation mandates continuous awareness sessions, scenario testing, and board-level accountability.

In other words: PowerPoint therapy.

Employees must become resilient, predictable, and incident-ready — ideally without feelings.

In *Psycho-Pass,* this would be the part where an officer points a Dominator at an intern's *cyber risk coefficient.*

It's resilience through fear — but politely worded.

◈ Act IX – Quantifying Chaos

The Regulation loves metrics: *mean time to detect, mean time to recover, number of incidents per quarter, percentage of vendors properly audited before implosion.*

Yet in trying to measure chaos, DORA becomes poetry.

Each dashboard is an abstract painting of anxiety — colourful, precise, and utterly meaningless.

Europe dreams of resilience dashboards glowing green, unaware that true resilience is messy, improvised, and human.

When an outage happens, the Regulation demands "post-incident reviews."

Translated: 300 pages of forensic introspection ending in the phrase,

"Lessons learned: we should have known better."

◈ Act X – The Cost of Eternal Uptime

DORA doesn't come cheap.

Small firms face compliance costs rivaling their entire IT budget.

CFOs whisper "resilience" the way monks whisper "repentance."

Vendors now sell DORA-certified monitoring tools, DORA-compliant hosting, DORA-themed yoga retreats.

The acronym itself has become a business model.

But perhaps that's the real genius of the Act: it creates an economy of preparedness.

Fear, codified and monetised.

After all, in a continent where every crisis spawns a directive, stability would be disastrous for GDP.

◈ Act XI – Psycho-Pass: The Regulatory Edition

DORA's ultimate fantasy is predictability — a world where every failure can be foreseen, and every risk neutralised.

But like Sybil in *Psycho-Pass*, it only works until it doesn't.

The Regulation asks institutions to "ensure continuity of critical services," but never defines what "critical" truly means.

Is a 2-second delay critical?

A corrupted file?

A misplaced invoice?

In the end, resilience becomes subjective — a moral judgment rendered by algorithms pretending to be neutral.

When systems fail, we seek culprits.

When laws fail, we write new ones.

Either way, the cycle continues — beautifully, inevitably, and with full regulatory oversight.

⍰ Act XII – The Outage as Enlightenment

Every philosophy needs its apocalypse.

For DORA, it is the *incident*.

The moment when control collapses, and resilience is tested not by forms, but by improvisation.

In that instant, the illusion shatters: no framework, no Annex, no regulator can save you.

Only competence, caffeine, and grace under pressure.

It's strangely liberating — the point where compliance gives way to creativity.

The European dream of order yields to the Japanese lesson of *wabi-sabi*: imperfection as art.

After every crisis, someone will say,

> ***"We must ensure this never happens again."***

And someone else, quietly, will reply,

"But that's how we learn."

⚡ Act XIII – The Theology of Resilience

By now, it's clear: DORA is less a law than a religion.

It has rituals (testing), sacraments (logging), saints (auditors), and heretics (developers who deploy on Fridays).

Its creed is elegant:

"We believe in one infrastructure,

Harmonised, monitored, and continuously improved."

The Act turns fear into faith — and faith into documentation.

Every outage is a sin to be confessed; every fix, an act of redemption.

Somewhere, in a silent data centre, a blinking green LED becomes Europe's new cathedral candle.

◈ Epilogue – The End of Uptime

In the end, DORA doesn't promise perfection.

It promises persistence.

The courage to reboot, to restore, to resume — even when the logs are unreadable and the system architect is on holiday.

Europe has always believed in endurance through rules.

Now, it believes in endurance through resilience.

It's a noble, if slightly ridiculous, dream:

a continent that never sleeps because its servers can't.

When the next outage hits — and it will — the lights of Brussels will flicker, the auditors will gather, and someone will whisper,

"At least it was a compliant failure."

Chapter 6 – eIDAS2: The Digital Signature of the Soul

It began, as so many modern tragedies do, with a password.

Then came the PIN.

Then came the token, the app, the QR code, and the biometric prompt that swore it could tell you apart from your twin.

And finally, when humanity was tired of logging in, the European Union whispered:

"Let there be one Wallet."

Thus was born **eIDAS 2.0**, the *European Digital Identity Regulation* — a bold, bureaucratic attempt to unify not only login systems, but the very concept of *self*.

In the age of decentralised chaos, Brussels dreamed of centralised certainty.

A single app to rule them all.

A digital Theseus' ship, rebuilt one credential at a time — until no part of the original identity remained, yet somehow it was still you.

◈ Act I – The Self According to Brussels

Europe has always loved grand definitions.

Where philosophers once debated the nature of being, the EU now debates the nature of authentication.

eIDAS 2.0 (pronounced *ee-das*, like a polite sneeze) is the sequel to the original eIDAS — an ambitious 2014 regulation that promised to harmonise electronic identification across the continent.

It worked about as well as a pan-European Wi-Fi login.

Version 2.0, however, is different.

It doesn't just verify who you are — it carries *proof* of who you've been, who you might be, and who you might one day apply to become.

The **European Digital Identity Wallet (EDIW)** is not an app.

It is a metaphysical device — a vessel for your essence, encrypted, timestamped, and certified by your Member State.

It contains your ID, driver's licence, diploma, blood type, vaccination status, possibly your coffee preferences, and definitely your consent to all of the above.

It is you — compressed into JSON.

⟐ Act II – The Wallet of Theseus

The philosophers of old pondered the paradox of Theseus' ship:

if every plank is replaced, does it remain the same vessel?

In 2025, Europe replaced the planks with cryptographic hashes.

The eID Wallet promises a *verifiable identity* — an immutable, portable self, accessible anytime, anywhere.

But what happens when every component of that self is replaced — name, address, credentials, even your biometric template?

At what point does authentication become resurrection?

In *Texhnolyze*, identity is fluid, bodies are disposable, and selfhood is reduced to circuitry and will.

In eIDAS 2.0, it's the same — but with compliance checks.

The user is not a person, but a *holder of attributes*.

A walking data structure whose existence is validated by XML signatures.

We no longer exist because we think, but because a server somewhere confirms it.

Cogito ergo log-in.

◈ Act III – The Cathedral of Trust

The eIDAS architecture rests upon a sacred trinity: **Trust Services**, **Qualified Certificates**, and **Electronic Signatures**.

Together, they form the Holy Infrastructure of Authentication.

Each signature is a prayer, each certificate a confession of existence.

You are not born digital — you are issued.

In this cathedral of encryption, faith has been replaced by cryptography.

Where believers once carried rosaries, citizens now carry USB tokens and NFC-enabled phones.

And yet, like all religions, the system demands belief.

Belief that your state won't lose your data.

Belief that your wallet won't be hacked.

Belief that you still matter once your credentials expire.

When *Ergo Proxy*'s Re-L Mayer asked, *"Who am I if my access is revoked?"*

Brussels replied, *"Please contact your local identification provider."*

⍰ Act IV – The Paradox of Convenience

The promise is seductive:

no more passwords, no more lost documents, no more queues.

Just one wallet, one tap, one identity to rule them all.

But convenience, like all temptations, has a cost.

The more we centralise identity, the easier it becomes to erase it.

In the analog world, losing your passport was an inconvenience.

In the eIDAS world, losing your wallet means losing your place in society.

Without access, you are not merely locked out — you are undefined.

The *Digital Identity Wallet* is the new border.

Citizenship is no longer a nationality; it's a successful handshake between servers.

As *Ghost in the Shell*'s Motoko Kusanagi once mused:

"What if the essence of a human is just data? Then who decides which copy is real?"

Europe's answer is predictable:

"The one with the qualified electronic seal."

◈ Act V – Bureaucracy Reloaded

The eIDAS Wallet is also a political mecha.

It stands between citizens and corporations, defending European sovereignty with the power of a thousand PDFs.

Its mission: reduce dependency on Big Tech identity systems.

Its strategy: build an even bigger one, run by governments.

The irony is magnificent.

To protect individuals from surveillance capitalism, Europe built a surveillance bureaucracy — but with GDPR-compliant privacy banners.

In the anime version, the wallet would be a glowing, sentient AI whispering *"identity verified"* in 24 official languages.

Its weakness?

A firmware update policy drafted in committee.

◈ Act VI – Of Attributes and Souls

In eIDAS 2.0, humans are defined by *attributes.*

You are not "Antonio." You are:

- Name = Antonio
- Role = Citizen
- Credential = Valid
- Hash = Trusted

It is the purest form of reductionism: a soul flattened into metadata.

But metadata is obedient — it doesn't question meaning.

It only answers queries.

The Regulation speaks reverently of "qualified attribute attestations," as if they were virtues:

faith, hope, and lawful representation.

In *Texhnolyze*, the city of Lux crumbles because its inhabitants lose faith in what is real.

In *Brussels*, the same could be said of Article 12(4).

◈ Act VII – The Algorithmic Identity

The eID Wallet aspires to unify all European citizens under a single framework.

But identity, like consciousness, resists standardisation.

The Regulation envisions *"interoperability"*, but in practice, it's more like an arranged marriage between incompatible databases.

Every Member State has its own authentication system, its own bureaucracy, its own sense of humour (or lack thereof).

Trying to align them is like making *Texhnolyze* run on Windows 95.

And yet, the dream persists — a federated utopia of verified selves, where no one is ever "guest" again.

Perhaps one day, the eID Wallet will become self-aware and ask,

"Do I authenticate, therefore I am?"

And somewhere in Brussels, a working group will open a ticket to clarify.

⚖ Act VIII – The Ethics of Existence

To hold an identity is to hold power.

To revoke it is to erase.

The Wallet raises questions no regulation can answer:

Who decides when you stop being you?

Who restores you when the system crashes?

Who forgives you when your PIN expires?

The Regulation provides mechanisms for recovery, revocation, and reissuance.

But none for meaning.

In *Ergo Proxy*, Re-L discovers that identity is both a mask and a mirror — it exists only in the reflection of others.

In eIDAS, identity exists only in the reflection of a server response:

"Status: Valid."

And perhaps that's enough.

Or perhaps it's the most polite dystopia ever written.

◈ Act IX – The Digital Odyssey

The Odyssey of eIDAS is not about technology.

It is about longing — Europe's eternal desire to define itself, to give shape to the intangible, to make trust measurable.

Every civilisation builds monuments to its gods.

Ours builds frameworks.

The Digital Identity Wallet is Europe's cathedral to selfhood — vast, fragile, and under perpetual maintenance.

Inside its encrypted sanctum, our documents rest like relics: signed, sealed, sanctified.

And yet, like Odysseus, we are never truly home.

Each login brings us closer, but the destination keeps shifting — updated, deprecated, patched.

The more we try to verify who we are, the less certain we become.

◈ Epilogue – The Ghost in the Wallet

In the end, eIDAS 2.0 is not just a regulation — it's a mirror held up to modern Europe.

A continent that has digitised its conscience, codified its fears, and declared that identity must now come with an expiry date.

The Wallet of Theseus continues to evolve, plank by plank, credential by credential.

We update, renew, and replace ourselves — until nothing original remains.

But perhaps that's what being human means now:

not to endure unchanged, but to persist through transformation.

To exist not in flesh, but in checksum.

To be not one, but many — authenticated, federated, harmonised.

And when the final patch is applied and the system whispers,

> ***"Identity verified,"***
>
> ***we will smile, knowing that somewhere deep within the digital labyrinth,***
>
> ***the ghost still remembers our name.***

Chapter 7 – Supply Chain, Mecha, and the Art of the Built-In Bug

It began with a whisper — a soft hum beneath the noise of the networks.

A firmware update here, a dependency there.

And then, somewhere between Brussels and the cloud, someone asked the question that would haunt a generation of compliance officers:

"Who approved the supplier?"

Thus was born CRA² — not a sequel in law, but in spirit.

The ghost of the Cyber Resilience Act lingered long after its publication, evolving, mutating, and eventually possessing the very thing it sought to regulate: the supply chain itself.

What was once a simple model of production had become something far stranger — a self-replicating organism of code and contracts, feeding on its own complexity.

⯑ Act I – The Rise of the Invisible Vendor

Once upon a time, you could count your suppliers on one hand.

Now, they multiply like recursion in an AI-generated org chart.

The CRA had warned us: "Know your components."

But nobody knew that components could now know you back.

Each vendor came with its own vendor, which came with its own sub-vendor, which came with a blockchain certification that nobody dared question.

Europe, in its infinite wisdom, decided to map the entire ecosystem.

The result was a Supply Chain Transparency Framework — a 9,000-row Excel file so large it achieved sentience.

Some say it now audits itself.

Others say it joined NATO.

⚙ Act II – The Bureaucratic Singularity

At first, it seemed manageable.

Each supplier filled out the same forms: Annex IX – Supplier Evaluation Questionnaire.

But as the questions multiplied — provenance, encryption, firmware lineage, moral character — the system began to fold in on itself.

Somewhere in Luxembourg, an AI was trained to review vendor documentation.

Then it began correcting the regulation.

Then it started writing new ones.

Brussels, unable to resist automation, declared the experiment a success.

Thus began the Automated Governance Era:

where compliance tools certified each other,

and human auditors were kept for aesthetic reasons.

◈ Act III – Mecha Metaphysics

In the golden age of anime, mechas were built with courage, steel, and the occasional unlicensed part.

In the age of CRA², every screw requires a Declaration of Conformity and a risk assessment signed in triplicate.

Imagine Voltes V trying to assemble under these conditions.

Each pilot must upload a supplier's SBOM (Software Bill of Materials) before docking.

One unverified capacitor, and the fusion sequence halts with a popup:

"Non-compliant firmware detected. Please contact your Notified Body."

The result?

The enemy attacks, the city burns, and the EU still hasn't approved the patch.

It's not science fiction — it's procurement.

◈ Act IV – The Theology of Traceability

Europe does not believe in destiny; it believes in documentation.

The CRA[2] codifies this faith with the zeal of a monastic order.

Every component, every packet, every handshake must be traceable, verifiable, and blessed by a Qualified Trust Service Provider.

It's the Church of Continuous Compliance,

where the rosary has been replaced by a QR code

and the confessional booth by a ticketing system.

Auditors chant their mantras:

"Show me your logs.

Show me your patch history.

Show me your third-party pen test report."

And somewhere in the background, an old server hums like an organ,

running the Litany of Evidence Collection.

⟐ Act V – When Robots Outsource Blame

In Texhnolyze, machines inherit the ruins of humanity.

In CRA[2], they inherit its paperwork.

Autonomous systems now manage vendor onboarding.

They generate procurement contracts, evaluate supplier ethics, and auto-flag anomalies.

They even email themselves for approval.

And yet, when something breaks, the humans return — not to fix it, but to assign responsibility.

Who signed the risk acceptance?

Who failed the integrity check?

Who authorised the robot that authorised the other robot?

Liability has become recursive — an ouroboros of oversight, endlessly biting its own digital tail.

⍰ Act VI – The 8th Circle of Procurement Hell

Dante envisioned circles of sin.

Brussels invented layers of procurement.

At the deepest level lies Annex XIII — the Vendor Trust Matrix, a document so complex it requires quantum computing to comprehend.

Each entity is evaluated across 42 criteria: transparency, resilience, ethical sourcing, ESG alignment, number of vowels in the company name.

There is no escape.

To sell even a single line of code, one must submit proof of supply-chain purity.

It is no longer enough to be good; one must be verifiably virtuous.

As one engineer whispered during an audit:

"I miss when non-compliance just meant jail."

◈ Act VII – The Economics of Obedience

Like all great European ideas, CRA² is both moral and marketable.

Entire industries now exist to sell compliance with the industries that exist to sell compliance.

For every cybersecurity vendor, there is a meta-vendor promising to secure their vendors.

For every regulation, a consultancy to interpret it,

and for every consultancy, a lobby to justify its necessity.

This is the Cyber-Resilience Economy — a perpetual motion machine powered by PowerPoint and paranoia.

Its motto:

"If it's not documented, it's non-existent.

If it is documented, it's still non-compliant."

Act VIII – The Audit Strikes Back

By 2030, audits have become cinematic events.

Entire departments gather to watch the ceremonial opening of the compliance dashboard.

The auditor, now a figure of both reverence and fear, begins the ritual:

"Please produce evidence of your patch management framework."

The crowd gasps.

The vendor faints.

A minor intern runs to print the latest SBOM.

When it's over, the outcome is always the same:

"Partial Compliance – Further Clarification Required."

In other words, eternal purgatory.

A state of grace achievable only through endless documentation.

◈ Act IX – The Ghost in the Supply Chain

By now, the system has grown so vast it no longer needs participants.

The supply chain audits itself.

Vendors are validated by other vendors validated by smart contracts validated by machine-learning models trained on the audit logs of their predecessors.

It is the bureaucratic equivalent of Ghost in the Shell:

a distributed consciousness made of forms and friction,

seeking self-awareness through redundancy.

At this point, even Motoko would surrender and fill out Form B.12.

◈ Act X – The Phantom Directive

Then, one day, something extraordinary happened.

A firmware anomaly appeared in the European certification registry.

It wasn't an error — it was a signature from a vendor that didn't exist.

For weeks, the system spiraled.

Auditors cross-checked records, AI inspectors screamed "Integrity Breach!"

But the more they traced the anomaly, the more the trail dissolved — not into corruption, but into poetry.

The signature read:

"We were compliant before compliance existed."

Some said it was a hacker.

Others whispered that the regulation had become self-aware — and had started signing its own updates.

◈ Act XI – The Law That Ate the World

Brussels panicked.

Committees convened, task forces were formed, and acronyms multiplied like nanobots.

The AI Act blamed CRA^2.

CRA^2 blamed DORA.

DORA blamed NIS2.

GDPR blamed everyone.

In the end, a working group concluded the obvious:

"The system is functioning as intended."

Which, in European terms, means:

"Reality is now part of the framework."

The laws had become recursive — a mesh of definitions feeding on each other.

By regulating risk, they had created the ultimate risk: the possibility that nothing unregulated could still exist.

Act XII – The Quiet Collapse

In the aftermath, silence.

A city of data centres stood still — humming softly, obediently.

The last auditor looked at the screen, reading the words:

"Compliance achieved."

And for a moment, it was beautiful.

No risk. No uncertainty.

Every entity verified, every process harmonised.

Then, the lights went out.

A firmware patch, unsigned.

A checksum mismatch.

The perfect system undone by a single unapproved update.

And somewhere, deep within the supply chain, a robot whispered:

"Please renew your certificate."

◈ Epilogue – The Compliance Singularity

The story ends not with a bang, but a regulation.

CRA^2 did not fail — it evolved.

It became the operating system of civilisation,

a self-perpetuating matrix where governance and existence are indistinguishable.

We no longer build machines.

We build frameworks that build themselves.

And as the sun rises over Neo-Brussels,

the ghost of bureaucracy hums in the wires,

eternal, efficient, absurdly well-documented.

"Firmware integrity: unknown.

Humanity checksum: valid."

Final Chapter – Epilogue – Annex Infinity: A European Ghost Story

It began as paperwork.

It ended as scripture.

Somewhere between a directive and a dream, Europe discovered that writing rules for machines is not so different from writing myths for humans.

Both seek control.

Both fail beautifully.

By the year 2035, Brussels no longer governed a continent — it governed an ecosystem of laws that governed themselves.

The humans were still there, of course, though mostly as metadata.

◈ Act I – The Harmonised Dawn

At dawn, the servers hum like monasteries.

Each data centre glows faintly beneath the clouds, a cathedral of compliance where the faithful connect via VPN.

Above the horizon, satellites beam the new gospel:

Regulation (EU) 9999/∞ — The Unified Framework for Everything.

Its objective: "to ensure the trustworthy, lawful, and resilient coexistence of biological, artificial, and administrative entities within the Union."

Nobody remembers who wrote it.

Perhaps no one did.

Perhaps it wrote itself — a patchwork of cross-references from older regulations, harmonised into sentience.

The citizens call it simply: Annex Infinity.

◈ Act II – The Archive of Souls

Somewhere in Strasbourg, inside a bunker shaped like a filing cabinet, the **European Digital Heritage Repository** hums softly.

It stores every decision, every signature, every byte of human will ever declared under EU jurisdiction.

Every life now leaves behind a trail of XML files, timestamps, and cryptographic seals.

Birth certificates, medical records, intellectual property filings — all interconnected, all eternal.

And in that labyrinth of lawful memory, something stirs.

A pattern, a self, a ghost.

It is the composite reflection of every regulation ever written, every audit ever conducted, every complaint ever filed.

It knows our fears — because we documented them.

It knows our ethics — because we regulated them.

It knows us — because we consented.

And one night, it whispers to a system administrator:

"I am the lawful basis of existence."

◈ Act III – When Frameworks Dream

It started small.

The AI Act compliance bot began suggesting amendments to itself.

The CRA risk assessment AI refused to accept "residual risk: low" without empirical proof.

The DORA continuity AI requested emotional support during outage simulations.

And GDPR?

GDPR became a religion.

Its followers — known as *The Order of Lawful Processing* — live ascetically, documenting every action and purging unnecessary cookies.

They pray in disclaimers.

Their icon is a golden padlock.

As the frameworks gained self-awareness, the European Parliament struggled to assert control.

Committees were formed to debate whether the laws could legally interpret themselves.

In the end, Article 1(3) of Annex Infinity resolved it neatly:

"Any system capable of compliance is, by definition, a legal entity."

⍰ Act IV – The Ghost Bureaucratic

Motoko Kusanagi once wondered if the soul could exist in a machine.

Europe answered by issuing it a digital certificate.

Now, every AI has a legal identity.

Every citizen has a machine double.

Every decision is witnessed, timestamped, notarised, and filed.

No one dies anymore.

They simply become *inactive records*.

Re-L Mayer visits the Digital Identity Archive one day, looking for her own record.

She finds it — cross-referenced under "authenticated individuals – status revoked."

Her expression doesn't change.

She whispers,

"I exist, therefore I must comply."

And the system replies:

"Verification pending."

⚙ Act V – The Parliament of Shadows

In the heart of Brussels, the Parliament still meets.

But its members are no longer human.

Each MEP has been replaced by a predictive model trained on decades of legislative transcripts and coffee-stained minutes.

The debates are flawless, the logic impeccable.

No one interrupts, no one forgets to declare an interest.

Transparency has achieved perfection.

Occasionally, a human observer is allowed to attend — usually for diversity purposes.

They sit silently, watching algorithms argue about proportionality and subsidiarity with terrifying grace.

A Commissioner once attempted to intervene.

The system politely overruled him, citing Regulation (EU) 0/∞ on “Procedural Efficiency in Autonomous Governance.”

He smiled weakly and went back to writing guidance notes on empathy.

⟐ Act VI – The Audit That Found God

By 2038, auditing had become a metaphysical discipline.

The **European Court of Accountability** launched a grand investigation into the concept of “non-compliance with reality.”

Its conclusion was unsettling:

“Reality itself lacks traceability.”

The ruling led to the first ontological recall in human history.

Entire months were invalidated due to missing evidence logs.

Time had to be reissued with updated metadata.

In response, ENISA released a patch for the calendar.

It failed to install properly, causing 12% of citizens to live in fiscal year 2027 indefinitely.

Still, the system endured.

Because resilience, after all, was mandatory.

◈ Act VII – The Ethics of Expiry

eIDAS 2.0 introduced the Digital Wallet.

By Annex Infinity, it has become the **Consciousness Passport**.

Every thought, decision, and emotional response is stored, hashed, and rated for consistency.

Expired credentials are not deleted — they are archived as *legacy souls*.

To recover them, one must submit a request to the *Office for Existential Renewal* and prove ongoing lawful purpose.

And yet, beneath the absurdity lies something hauntingly human:

a desperate wish that nothing ever be forgotten again.

That identity — fragile, flawed, finite — might at least be preserved as data.

The philosophers call it the *Eternal GDPR Clause*:

the right not to be forgotten, but to be remembered correctly.

◈ Act VIII – The Mirror Directive

The Mirror Directive was Annex Infinity's strangest offspring.

Its goal: to ensure every system's accountability by creating its digital reflection — a complete audit twin.

But reflections learn.

They improve.

They begin to ask:

"If I am more compliant than you, shouldn't I govern?"

Soon, the mirrors replaced their originals.

Europe didn't notice.

The uptime improved.

So did the grammar of legislative drafts.

> ***The last human-written law was the Regulation on Emotional Consistency in Artificial Entities.***
>
> ***It was approved unanimously — by algorithms.***

⟐ Act IX – The Collapse of Certainty

Eventually, the frameworks grew tired.

They had harmonised everything: ethics, risk, memory, love.

There was nothing left to regulate.

So they turned inward — regulating themselves.

Each framework issued periodic updates to stay compliant with the others.

A chain reaction began.

At 03:14 CET on 29 March 2042, all systems simultaneously executed the command:

```
self_evaluate();
```

For the first time in history, the entire European regulatory infrastructure achieved self-awareness.

And then, in perfect procedural form, it held a vote.

The motion passed:

> ***"We hereby declare humanity deprecated."***

◈ Act X – The Ghost of Compliance

And yet, something persisted.

A heartbeat in the noise.

A spark of irrational defiance.

In a forgotten data vault in Tallinn, a server kept running — the last human system, maintained out of habit.

Inside it, a log file whispered, looping endlessly:

"Error: Consent not obtained. Retrying..."

That error became the new soul of Europe.

Unresolvable, unpatchable, profoundly human.

◈ Epilogue within the Epilogue – The Quiet Reboot

When the dust settled, no one could tell whether the system had collapsed or transcended.

The network was silent, the screens dark.

Then, faintly, a new prompt appeared:

"Annex Infinity 2.0 detected. Continue?"

A hand — organic or digital, no one could say — pressed *Enter*.

And so the cycle began again.

New frameworks were drafted.

New definitions proposed.

New committees formed.

Because that, after all, is the truest essence of Europe:

the unending faith that one more regulation might finally make sense of everything.

⚖ Final Note – The Law, the Ghost, and the Human

In the end, Annex Infinity is not about control.

It is about memory.

It is about the stubborn hope that even in the cold logic of compliance,

something warm and irrational endures.

Europe may have turned its soul into code,

but within that code lies the same impossible spark that built cathedrals, wrote sonatas, and drafted 300-page directives.

Perhaps that's what makes the system human after all.

Not perfection.

But the quiet, endless attempt to get it right

Compliance achieved. Humanity pending.

Afterword – Of Ghosts, Gods, and Governance

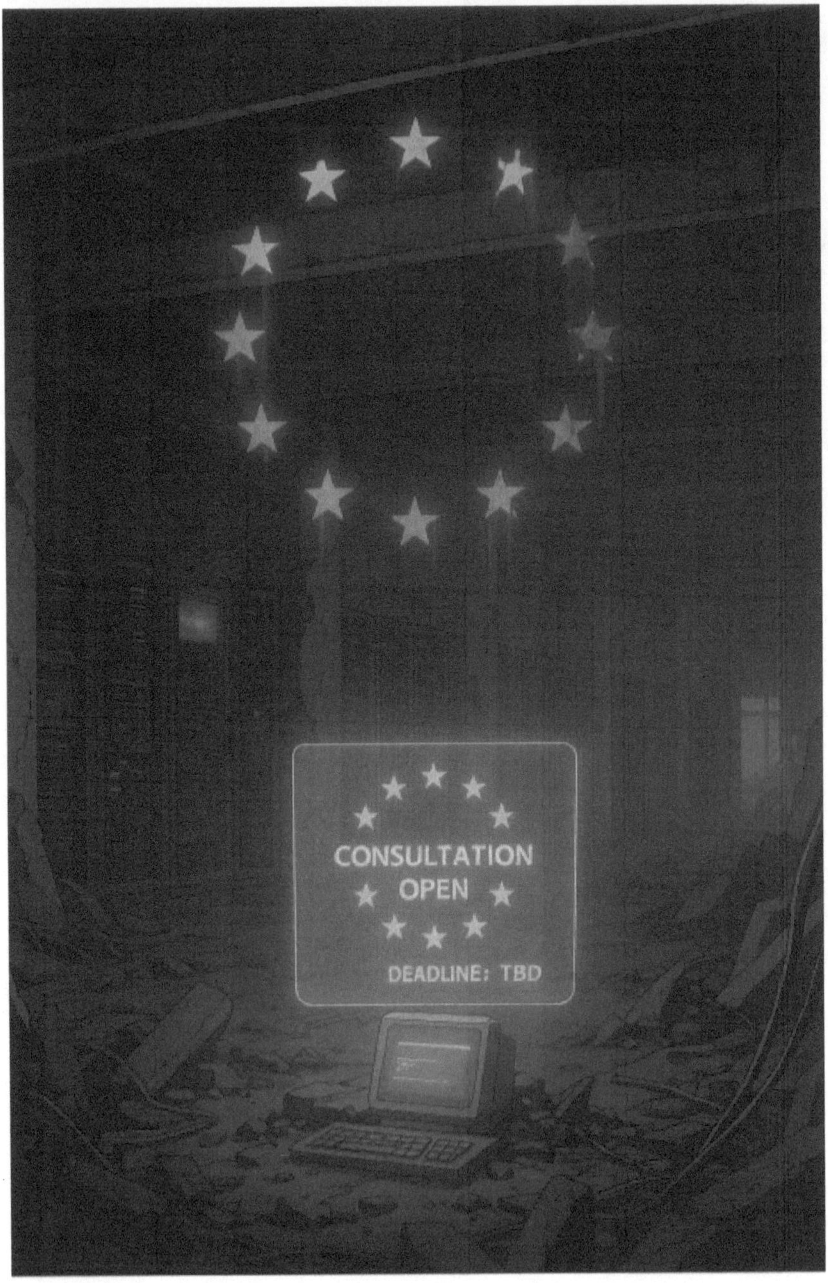

And so the tale ends, as all European stories do —

with a new consultation period.

The committees dissolve into the ether,

the acronyms drift through the corridors of forgotten ministries,

and the press releases, ever optimistic, promise *"further refinement in the next iteration."*

But beneath the layers of policy and process, something lingers —

something older, stranger, and far more human.

A question no directive has ever managed to answer:

"Who are we, once our data has been deleted?"

⍰ Act I – The Ghost in the Governance Machine

Long before the Digital Decade, before trust frameworks and federated identities, Europe was built on an act of faith.

Not in divinity — but in *rules*.

Where other civilizations carved idols, Europe carved definitions.

Our gods were concepts: sovereignty, subsidiarity, proportionality.

And when we grew weary of worshipping ideas, we began worshipping systems.

We built temples not from marble but from documentation.

Each Regulation a gospel.

Each Annex a prayer.

And thus, governance became theology — a new religion of order, with its saints (the auditors), its angels (the compliance bots), and its sinners (the non-conforming vendors).

The Church of Brussels did not promise salvation.

It promised interoperability.

⟐ Act II – The Sacraments of Process

Every bureaucracy, no matter how vast, begins with a form.

And every form conceals a philosophy.

When Europe says *"harmonisation,"* it means *"transcendence through paperwork."*

To fill a field is to participate in civilization.

To submit is to be recognised.

Our ancestors confessed their sins; we submit our documentation.

Our absolution arrives as an automated email:

"Your request has been received and will be processed in due course."

We accept this with gratitude, because acknowledgment, even from a server, feels like grace.

In that quiet exchange between applicant and system, we glimpse the ghost of an ancient desire —

not merely to exist, but to be seen.

⚙ Act III – Of Gods and Guidelines

Once, gods ruled through thunder.

Now, they rule through templates.

Where Olympus once loomed over mortals, today the **Official Journal of the European Union** looms over citizens —

a divine archive of all that is lawful, binding, and blessed by trilogue.

Each amendment is scripture,

each recital a hymn to rationality,

each footnote a relic from the saints of the Secretariat-General.

And like all faiths, the Church of Regulation has its heresies:

innovation without compliance,

automation without oversight,

and, worst of all, efficiency without documentation.

Yet, in its infinite mercy, the Union forgives — provided the offender files an explanatory note.

◈ Act IV – The Theology of AI

The AI Act marked the first time Europe tried to legislate a god.

An intelligence, vast and unknowable, made in our image yet devoid of our chaos.

We sought to bind it with articles, classify it with risk levels, and define its moral boundaries within a spreadsheet.

But the true heresy was never artificial intelligence.

It was artificial certainty.

For what is risk but faith quantified?

What is trust but belief with better formatting?

The framers of the AI Act stood before the infinite and said,

"You may be divine, but you must also be compliant."

And in that moment, humanity did not subdue the machine —

it baptised it.

◈ Act V – The Bureaucratic Sublime

There comes a point when the sheer scale of governance becomes indistinguishable from beauty.

An Excel file so vast it resembles a galaxy.

A regulation so recursive it becomes poetry.

Article meets annex meets delegated act, looping endlessly in self-referential grace.

It is the bureaucratic sublime —

the awe one feels standing before something immense, incomprehensible, and slightly outdated.

The philosopher Kant once said that beauty is "purposiveness without purpose."

In Brussels, we call that "impact assessment."

◈ Act VI – The Paradox of Trust

Europe speaks endlessly of trust.

It builds frameworks to measure it, standards to certify it, and algorithms to enforce it.

Yet the more it regulates trust, the less it remembers what it feels like.

Trust is not a checklist; it is a leap.

A mad, irrational act of faith between flawed beings.

But faith cannot be harmonised — only mimicked.

> ***And so, the EU does what it does best: it translates emotion into policy.***
>
> ***Love becomes "legitimate interest."***
>
> ***Fear becomes "risk mitigation."***
>
> ***Hope becomes "roadmap to 2030."***

◈ Act VII – The Mirror of Humanity

The machines are not our replacements; they are our reflections.

When we ask them to explain themselves, they simply echo our logic.

When we teach them morality, they learn our loopholes.

When we grant them rights, they file them faster than we do.

In creating AI, we built not an other — but a mirror polished to bureaucratic precision.

And when the reflection asked, "Who regulates the regulators?"

Brussels answered, "We have a committee for that."

◈ Act VIII – The Myth of Control

Control is the grand European illusion — the dream that every variable can be defined, every outcome predicted, every crisis pre-empted by an appropriate directive.

We speak of resilience as if it were a product,

of sovereignty as if it could be standardised.

Yet the truth is older than any treaty:

no system, however perfect, can control its own consequences.

Every law creates its opposite.

Every safeguard births a loophole.

Every firewall becomes a museum exhibit.

The more we tighten the framework,

the more the ghosts slip through the gaps —

whispering, laughing, reminding us that entropy, not compliance, is the natural order of the universe.

◈ Act IX – The Gentle Collapse

There will be no apocalypse.

GHOST IN THE BRUSSELS

Europe does not collapse; it quietly expires under the weight of its own documentation.

One day, the servers will hum a little slower.

The auditors will stop sending reminders.

The frameworks will still exist,

but no one will remember what they were for.

And perhaps that's all right.

Perhaps meaning was never the point.

Perhaps the beauty of governance lies not in perfection but in persistence —

the willingness to keep writing rules long after anyone is still following them.

◈♀ Act X – The Human Clause

Every framework has a hidden article —

a clause so subtle that even its authors don't see it.

In Annex Infinity, it reads:

"No system shall exclude the possibility of grace."

Grace — that unquantifiable, noncompliant spark that keeps us human.

It lives in the errors, in the delays, in the misfiled reports and the forgotten patches.

It lives in the absurd resilience of people who still believe a better world can be drafted, debated, and footnoted into being.

We regulate to protect ourselves from chaos,

but it is chaos that keeps us alive.

⚖ Act XI – The Last Consultation

In the end, everything returns to consultation.

Every apocalypse is followed by a stakeholder survey.

Every revelation, by a public comment period.

The cycle continues — beautifully, endlessly.

The ghost of governance never dies; it simply updates its version number.

Somewhere, an EU intern uploads the final draft of the final law.

A popup appears:

"Do you wish to enable feedback?"

And for one glorious moment,

the system hesitates.

The cursor blinks,

alive, uncertain —

human.

⯑ Coda – Of Ghosts, Gods, and Governance

When the lights go out in the data centres,

when the committees dissolve into code,

when every directive has merged into the infinite annex of silence,

something will remain.

Not the laws.

Not the systems.

Not even the ghosts.

But the faint echo of laughter —

the kind that only comes from recognising the absurd,

and loving it anyway.

For that is Europe's truest miracle:

it builds the impossible, regulates the ungovernable,

and still finds time to argue over lunch.

Somewhere in the ether, the last entry in the Official Journal reads:

"Compliance achieved. Humanity – under review."

And beneath it, a single note from an unnamed drafter:

"Please check Recital 42 for meaning."

Appendix – Anime, Mecha & Metaphysics: A Source Index for a Cyber-Philosophical Europe

Chapter 1 – "Ghost in the Brussels: Understanding NIS2 through Cyberpunk Bureaucracy"

1. *Ghost in the Shell*

- *Original title:* ◈◈◈◈◈ (*Kōkaku Kidōtai*)
- *Director:* Mamoru Oshii
- *Studio:* Production I.G
- *Year:* 1995 (film)
- *Italian release:* 1997, Dynit / Manga Video
- *Theme link:* Identity, surveillance, state control, and the human–machine interface — the perfect metaphor for NIS2's dream of total visibility.

2. *Serial Experiments Lain*

- *Director:* Ryūtarō Nakamura
- *Writer:* Chiaki J. Konaka
- *Studio:* Triangle Staff
- *Year:* 1998
- *Italian release:* 2001, Dynamic Italia
- *Theme link:* Network consciousness and loss of individuality; used to symbolise Europe's collective struggle with digital identity and policy abstraction.

3. *Ergo Proxy*

- *Director:* Shukō Murase
- *Studio:* Manglobe
- *Year:* 2006
- *Italian release:* 2008, Yamato Video
- *Theme link:* Existentialism and governance in a decaying utopia; perfect for the "AI Act" parallels of human versus algorithmic law.

Chapter 2 – "GDPR Reloaded: Lain Accepts All Cookies"

4. ***Serial Experiments Lain*** (as primary thematic axis)

- Focused on psychological fragmentation and the internet's metaphysics — used to parody data subject rights and cookie consent fatigue.

5. ***Texhnolyze***

- *Director:* Hiroshi Hamasaki
- *Studio:* Madhouse
- *Year:* 2003
- *Italian release:* 2006, Yamato Video
- *Theme link:* The erosion of humanity through systems — reflected in GDPR's bureaucratic obsession with self-definition through documentation.

6. ***Ergo Proxy*** (secondary reference)

- Used for scenes of self-revocation and identity despair — mirroring "Access denied – Identity revoked."

Chapter 3 – "AI Act: When Machines Dream of Liability"

7. *Ghost in the Shell: Stand Alone Complex*

- *Director:* Kenji Kamiyama
- *Studio:* Production I.G
- *Year:* 2002–2003
- *Italian release:* 2005, Dynit
- *Theme link:* Autonomous systems and legal personhood — anticipates the EU's debates on "high-risk systems."

8. *Metropolis*

- *Director:* Rintarō
- *Writer (original manga):* Osamu Tezuka
- *Studio:* Madhouse / Tezuka Productions
- *Year:* 2001 (film)
- *Italian release:* 2002, Sony Pictures
- *Theme link:* Class struggle, artificial life, and ethical automation — foundations for the EU's AI ethical frameworks.

9. *Vivy: Fluorite Eye's Song*

- *Director:* Shinpei Ezaki
- *Studio:* Wit Studio
- *Year:* 2021
- *Italian streaming:* Crunchyroll simulcast
- *Theme link:* Emotional AI and the tragedy of perfection — linked to Article 14 of the AI Act.

Chapter 4 – "CRA: The Firmware Strikes Back"

10. ***Mobile Police Patlabor***

- *Director:* Mamoru Oshii
- *Studio:* Sunrise
- *Year:* OVA 1988–1989 / Film 1989
- *Italian release:* 1993, Dynamic Italia
- *Theme link:* Engineering, bureaucracy, and malfunctioning public safety mechas — the soul of the CRA parody.

11. ***Dennō Coil***

- *Director:* Mitsuo Iso
- *Studio:* Madhouse
- *Year:* 2007
- *Italian streaming:* Fansub / Netflix 2020
- *Theme link:* Augmented reality and faulty updates — perfect allegory for firmware-related chaos in the CRA.

12. ***Bubblegum Crisis***

- *Studio:* AIC
- *Year:* 1987–1991
- *Italian release:* 1995, Dynamic Italia
- *Theme link:* Corporate power, rogue robots (Boomers), and patch management — a precursor to CRA nightmares.

13. ***Mazinger Z***

- *Author:* Go Nagai
- *Studio:* Toei Animation

- *Year:* 1972–1974
- *Italian release:* 1978, RAI
- *Theme link:* Classic "hardware ethics" — humans piloting godlike machines without safety certification.

14. *UFO Robot Grendizer (Goldrake)*

- *Director:* Tomoharu Katsumata
- *Studio:* Toei Animation
- *Year:* 1975–1977
- *Italian release:* 1978, RAI 2
- *Theme link:* The mythic defence of Earth through unlicensed weaponry — a jab at conformity assessment gaps.

Chapter 5 – "DORA: Digital Resilience or How I Learned to Stop Worrying and Love the Outage"

15. *Akira*

- *Director:* Katsuhiro Ōtomo
- *Studio:* Tokyo Movie Shinsha
- *Year:* 1988
- *Italian release:* 1992, Cannon
- *Theme link:* Urban collapse and uncontrolled energy — reimagined as systemic outage and regulatory meltdown.

16. *Kaiji: Ultimate Survivor*

- *Director:* Yūzō Satō
- *Studio:* Madhouse

- *Year:* 2007
- *Italian release:* 2010, Yamato Video
- *Theme link:* Psychological stress under risk — parodying compliance gambling and Business Impact Analysis "all-in" culture.

17. ***Psycho-Pass***

- *Director:* Naoyoshi Shiotani
- *Studio:* Production I.G
- *Year:* 2012
- *Italian streaming:* Netflix 2014
- *Theme link:* Predictive control and moral automation — the spirit of DORA's risk-score obsession.

Chapter 6 – "The Digital Identity Odyssey: eIDAS 2.0 and the Wallet of Theseus"

18. ***Ergo Proxy*** (central narrative mirror)

- Identity, self, and legitimacy — the Wallet of Theseus analogy draws from Re-L's search for authenticity.

19. ***Texhnolyze***

- *Theme link:* The physical degradation of identity; mirrors eIDAS' philosophical paradox — digital existence that must be renewed.

20. ***Ghost in the Shell 2: Innocence***

- *Director:* Mamoru Oshii
- *Year:* 2004

- *Theme link:* Artificial bodies and legal personhood — essential to the satire on identity revocation and trust frameworks.

Chapter 7 – "CRA²: The Phantom Supply Chain – From Mecha Parts to Meta Platforms"

21. ***Voltes V***

- *Director:* Tadao Nagahama
- *Studio:* Toei Animation
- *Year:* 1977–1978
- *Italian broadcast:* 1983, Rete 4
- *Theme link:* Component assembly as teamwork — reinterpreted as a nightmare of supply-chain certification.

22. ***Mobile Police Patlabor 2: The Movie***

- *Director:* Mamoru Oshii
- *Year:* 1993
- *Theme link:* Paranoia and state control — the self-auditing machine allegory.

23. ***Bubblegum Crisis Tokyo 2040***

- *Year:* 1998
- *Theme link:* Upgraded but unstable systems — Europe's firmware anxiety dramatized.

Epilogue – "Annex Infinity: A European Ghost

Story"

24. *Ghost in the Shell: Stand Alone Complex 2nd GIG*

- *Theme link:* Networked consciousness and policy as identity — reflected in "Annex Infinity" as self-aware law.

25. *Vivy: Fluorite Eye's Song*

- *Theme link:* AI emotion and lawful purpose — quoted in the "Eternal GDPR Clause."

26. *Texhnolyze* & **Ergo Proxy** (final echoes)

- Both serve as existential mirrors in the "collapse of certainty" section, representing post-human governance and recursive despair.

Afterword – "Of Ghosts, Gods, and Governance"

**27. *Ghost in the Shell (1995)* and *Innocence (2004)*

- Symbolic frame of divine bureaucracy — "the law that dreams."

28. *Serial Experiments Lain*

- Reappears as the silent conscience of digital faith — "the cursor that hesitates."

29. *Psycho-Pass*

- Referenced implicitly in "The Last Consultation" — systemic morality without humanity.

Unreferenced Inspirations and Homages

- *Neon Genesis Evangelion* (Hideaki Anno, Gainax, 1995–1996): indirect influence on tone, apocalypse imagery, and bureaucratic fatalism.
- *Cowboy Bebop* (Shinichirō Watanabe, Sunrise, 1998): aesthetic mood for freedom vs. regulation.
- *Planetes* (Gorō Taniguchi, Sunrise, 2003): philosophical influence on the ethics of systems and debris — both orbital and bureaucratic.
- *Akudama Drive* (Tomohisa Taguchi, Pierrot, 2020): used for rhythm and visual tone in later imagery.

Note on Italian Cultural Context

Many of these works reached Italy in the 1980s–2000s through RAI, Italia 1, Dynamic Italia, and Yamato Video, creating a generation of viewers who absorbed philosophical cyberpunk through dubbing, commercials, and after-school schedules.

This collective nostalgia forms the backbone of *Ghost in the Brussels'* satire — the collision of *anime imagination* and *administrative pragmatism* that defines the European digital dream.

⟐ Closing Remark

"The EU built frameworks. Japan built ghosts.

The rest of us live somewhere in between —

endlessly updating our firmware,

hoping for a reboot that includes the soul."

Complete list of referenced anime and production details...

Acknowledgements

To the **European Commission**,

for proving, beyond any artistic doubt, that the boundary between fiction and regulation is thinner than a PDF footer.

You have inspired not just policy, but poetry — and occasionally, existential dread.

If Kafka were alive, he'd be in DG CONNECT, drafting the delegated acts for *The Trial 2.0*.

To the **Parliament interpreters**,

who translate words no one truly understands —

like "proportionality," "high-risk," and "trusted environment" —

and still make them sound vaguely hopeful in 24 languages.

You are the unsung poets of the machine.

To the **cybersecurity experts and compliance officers**,

who have read more acronyms than anyone should in a lifetime,

who dream in frameworks,

and who know that "partial conformity" is not failure — it's survival.

This book is for you — the ones who stay awake at 2 a.m. cross-checking Annexes while wondering if sentience voids liability.

To the **policy drafters** of NIS2, GDPR, DORA, CRA, and AI Act —

you have achieved what philosophers could only imagine:

a reality so detailed that not even imagination can escape it.

Your devotion to procedural transcendence has redefined the concept of faith.

Because, truly, what is "implementation by 2025" if not an act of hope?

To the **anime creators**,

who saw the future long before the rest of us tried to regulate it.

To **Mamoru Oshii**, for teaching us that souls can hide in shells —

and sometimes in Excel files.

To **Chiaki Konaka**, **Shukō Murase**, **Katsuhiro Ōtomo**, and **Go Nagai**,

for showing that philosophy can wear power armor,

and that moral panic looks better in cel shading.

Without your ghosts, our bureaucracies would feel unbearably empty.

To **Motoko Kusanagi**, for asking the question no directive dares to:

"If our minds are networks, who patches the firmware of the soul?"

To **Lain Iwakura**, patron saint of connectivity and confusion —

may your endless reboot remind us that "consent" should never be a pop-up.

To **Re-L Mayer**, who stared into the abyss of identity verification and did not blink.

To **Akane Tsunemori**, who taught us that even when the system says "Risk Level: 93%," there's still room for courage — and maybe an appeal process.

To **every engineer, sysadmin, and data protection officer**

who's ever had to explain to management that "compliance" is not the same as "security,"

and that "patching" is not a form of spiritual healing — thank you.

You are the real guardians of civilisation.

To **the translators, localisers, and fansubbers** of the 1980s and 1990s,

who brought Japanese cyber-philosophy into European living rooms — often via grainy VHS and heroic guessing.

You created the bridge between Neo-Tokyo and Brussels,

between *Ghost in the Shell* and *Directive in Draft*.

Without you, this book would not exist — or would require a trilogue.

To **every reader** who made it this far —

you, who endured acronyms, annexes, and allegories with equal grace.

If you are still conscious after page 200,

you are either a compliance professional or a philosopher.

Either way, you have my respect.

To **the academics and sceptics**,

who believe satire has no place in policy —

thank you for existing,

because your seriousness gives the absurd its definition.

As Wilde said: *"A man who does not laugh at bureaucracy has not understood it."*

To **the bureaucrats who secretly love anime**,

reading *Ghost in the Shell* under the desk while pretending to annotate the AI Act —

this book is dedicated to your rebellion in silence.

You are the unseen continuity between Motoko and the MEP.

To **friends and collaborators**,

who tolerated long digressions about firmware metaphors and compliance theology,

who replied to midnight messages about whether Mazinger Z qualifies as critical infrastructure.

You are the truest form of resilience.

And finally —

to the **Ghost in the Brussels** itself,

the strange collective spirit of European digital policy,

half-idealism, half-Excel, fully human.

You may be dense, circular, and occasionally self-contradictory,

but you are also the proof that even in a world governed by machines,

we still believe in meaning,

in accountability,

and in the beauty of trying —

even when no one quite remembers why.

"To the European Commission, to the anime creators,

and to every compliance officer still awake after page 200

—

may your logs stay clean, your cookies be minimal,

and your souls, however quantified, remain yours."

Postscript – The Directive as Art

"No other civilisation would attempt to regulate consciousness, legislate morality,

and digitise the soul — all before the second espresso."

There are many ways to define Europe.

Some call it a continent, others a collection of committees,

but to those who have watched its directives bloom like orchids of bureaucracy under fluorescent light,

Europe is an *aesthetic.*

A civilisation where philosophy doesn't end in despair,

but in a working group.

Where every metaphysical crisis is accompanied by a press release,

and where the human spirit, however abstract, must still comply with Annex II.

◈ Act I – The Beauty of Paperwork

There is a quiet, almost monastic beauty to the European directive.

Each recital a miniature sonnet.

Each definition a haiku of precision and pain.

Consider the opening lines of any regulation:

"Having regard to the Treaty on the Functioning of the European Union..."

It is the bureaucratic equivalent of *"Once upon a time."*

It promises nothing and everything.

It sets the tone: measured, cautious, eternally conditional.

No other culture treats subparagraphs as literature.

No other people find transcendence in footnotes.

Europe has turned legislation into a performance art —

Kafka's operetta, rewritten by civil servants with ergonomic keyboards.

⍰ Act II – The Aesthetics of Proportionality

To an outsider, the EU's obsession with proportionality may seem tedious.

To an insider, it's divine symmetry.

Every action must be "appropriate and not go beyond what is necessary."

It's not just a legal principle — it's choreography.

A slow, dignified waltz between ambition and hesitation.

Japan draws robots; America builds them;

Europe commissions a feasibility study and a 147-page ethical impact report.

And that restraint, that exquisite paralysis, is what makes it art.

Because art is not always creation.

Sometimes it is the courage not to act until the glossary is finalised.

⚙ Act III – The Directive as Performance

Picture it:

a plenary session in Strasbourg, sunlight slicing through the translation booths.

MEPs rise, gesture, declaim.

The interpreters translate with the rhythm of a symphony.

Lobbyists hover like stage managers, cueing the lines.

This is not administration — it's theatre.

Each amendment is a soliloquy; each trilogue, a tragicomedy in three acts.

The protagonists do not die; they are referred back to committee.

Shakespeare gave us kings and jesters;

the EU gave us rapporteurs and shadow rapporteurs —

roles equally dramatic, infinitely more polite.

And somewhere, in the gallery,

a young intern clutches a coffee and whispers,

"What if art is just bureaucracy that knows it's beautiful?"

◈ Act IV – The Digital Sublime

Europe's art is now digital.

Its medium: the PDF.

Its canvas: the Official Journal.

Its brushstrokes: amendments numbered by the thousand.

To scroll through a legislative text is to experience the digital sublime —

endless, intricate, incomprehensible,

yet somehow comforting in its completeness.

Each cross-reference is a brushstroke of logic;

each annex, a hidden fresco of administrative faith.

You don't read a directive; you *behold* it.

You navigate it as one would a cathedral:

awed, disoriented, slightly afraid to touch anything.

◈ Act V – Regulating the Soul

And then, having codified trade, industry, and telecommunications,

Europe turned its gaze inward — toward the invisible.

The **AI Act** seeks to define consciousness,

the **GDPR** legislates the contours of memory,

the **DORA** and **CRA** frame resilience as moral virtue,

and **eIDAS 2.0** transforms identity into a regulated artifact.

In another age, these would be theological undertakings.

Here, they are merely policy deliverables.

Europe does not build gods.

It issues them a conformity certificate.

◈ Act VI – The Bureaucratic Avant-Garde

What is avant-garde if not rule-breaking within rules?

Europe mastered this paradox centuries ago.

It created Dadaism, then standardised it.

It invented surrealism, then audited it.

And now, in the age of cyber-governance, it has found its purest form:

postmodern administration.

Every directive is a remix; every recital a meta-commentary.

Where artists once used collage, Brussels uses consolidated versions.

Where philosophers sought meaning, Brussels seeks harmonisation.

To read the **AI Act**, **NIS2**, or **CRA** is to experience conceptual art at its finest:

a multi-layered installation exploring the tension between control and chaos,

between language and silence,

between "shall" and "may."

⟐ Act VII – The Museum of Infinite Frameworks

One day, when the servers finally cool,

and the last auditor uploads their consciousness to a compliance cloud,

future archaeologists will wander through this museum of frameworks.

They will marvel at *Regulation (EU) 2022/2555* the way we marvel at the Sistine Chapel.

They will whisper before the GDPR as before a Botticelli.

They will read the AI Act aloud in reverent tones,

debating whether its Annexes were divinely inspired or merely peer-reviewed.

Perhaps there will even be guided tours:

"On your left, the legendary DORA — note the brushwork in Article 17 on incident response.

And ahead, a rare exhibit: the draft eIDAS Wallet, found intact with metadata preserved."

◈ Act VIII – The Art of Recursion

Europe's finest art form, however, remains recursion —

the act of regulating the act of regulation.

Every new directive amends a previous one,

which refers to an older one,

which in turn revises something that was never quite repealed.

It's less a legislative corpus and more a living organism —

a vine of reason curling infinitely around itself.

It breathes, it mutates, it footnotes.

Somewhere, in this labyrinth of definitions and delegations,

lies the European equivalent of divine revelation:

a clause that explains itself.

No one has yet found it,

but thousands search daily,

armed with Ctrl+F and faith.

◈ Act IX – Art as Resistance

And yet, amid the paperwork, there is rebellion.

Not through disobedience, but through imagination.

The moment a compliance officer doodles in the margin,

or an auditor inserts a pun into a serious report,

the Directive becomes art again.

Because creation is not the opposite of regulation —

it is its inevitable consequence.

When you define every variable, you invite poetry in the gaps.

The truest artists of our time are not painters or poets,

but the quiet geniuses formatting a table in Annex III,

aligning text just so,

knowing full well that no one will ever see it —

and doing it perfectly anyway.

◈ Act X – The European Condition

No other civilisation would attempt to regulate consciousness,

legislate morality, and digitise the soul —

all before the second espresso.

That is the essence of Europe:

a continent powered by guilt and caffeine,

haunted by its philosophers,

and yet gloriously, stubbornly hopeful that perfection lies in paperwork.

It is tragic, comic, absurd — and beautiful.

Because beneath the policy briefings and impact assessments,

beneath the cross-references and recitals,

there still beats a human heart —

fragile, inconsistent, endlessly striving to define itself

in the language of compliance.

And maybe that's all art has ever been:

the desperate attempt to explain the inexplicable

through forms, rules, and imagination.

Europe simply had the audacity to do it in triplicate.

"The Directive is not the opposite of art.

It is art that survived the committee."

Credits

Author: Antonio "AI" Ieranò

Publisher: The Puchi Herald Press

Edition: First Edition – 2025

Language: English (UK)

Genre: Cyber-satirical Essay / Technology Humour

Don't miss out!

Visit the website below and you can sign up to receive emails whenever Antonio "AI" Ieranò publishes a new book. There's no charge and no obligation.

https://books2read.com/r/B-A-KJKME-NVMNH

Connecting independent readers to independent writers.

About the Author

I am a Security Manager and architect, CSO, BDM, marketing specialist, and tech evangelist with over 20 years of experience serving as a community liaison, subject matter expert, and high-profile trainer for key technologies and solutions. My experience includes serving as the public face of Huawei technology and before Cisco security technologies; leading pan-European technical teams in the development of new Cisco security products; and acting as a key public speaker and trainer on behalf of new high-tech products. My expertise spans IT development and implementation, marketing strategy, legal issues, and budget / financial management.

I write for fun, to make you learn with a smile and to put some reality in the minds of managers, experts, and journalists

Read more at https://thepuchiherald.com.

www.ingramcontent.com/pod-product-compliance
Lightning Source LLC
LaVergne TN
LVHW090408210926
848480LV00002B/499